Writing Teacher's Handbook
Expressive Writing

Written by June Hetzel and Deborah McIntire

A Poem
Student Author: Rachel Cech

A poem starts in the back of your head,
And you don't even know it's there.
It works its way to the front of your brain,
And seems to pop out of thin air!

A poem with people and places and things,
That tells about joy and despair.
That poem did start in the back of your head,
And you didn't know it was there!

Illustrator: Corbin Hillam
Editor: Joel Kupperstein
Project Director: Carolea Williams

CTP ©1998, Creative Teaching Press, Inc., Cypress, CA 90630

Table of Contents

Introduction

Expressive Writing is one resource in the *Writing Teacher's Handbook* four-book series that assists teachers of grades 4–6 in effectively implementing classroom writing programs. The lessons in each book include actual writing samples from upper-grade students.

Writing Domains

Each resource book in the *Writing Teacher's Handbook* series describes detailed lessons in one of the four writing domains—narrative, expressive, informative, and persuasive.

The *expressive domain* includes poems and stories that express sensory detail and emotions (e.g., journal entries, haiku). The *narrative domain* focuses on telling a story (e.g., autobiographical incidents, short stories). The *persuasive domain* involves convincing readers of beliefs and reasoning (e.g., persuasive essays, editorial comments). The *informative domain* encompasses writing products that explain factual information (e.g., research papers, reports).

Many writing products fall within more than one domain. For example, a ballad describes a person's emotions (expressive) but also tells a story (narrative). A dialogue can evoke emotion (expressive), but can also comprise the content of an interview (informative). Emphasize the critical components of each writing product to help your students sharpen their writing skills and prepare them for writing success.

Lesson Plan Format

Lessons in this book include:
Critical Components—a list of the essential components of each writing product
Preparation—a description of what teachers need to do prior to the lesson
Setting the Stage—hints for introducing the lesson and engaging student interest
Instructional Input—directions for initiating a formal writing lesson and modeling the critical components of writing samples
Guided Practice—exercises for reinforcing the writing lesson
Independent Practice—activities to help students write independently
Presentation—ideas for organizing, publishing, and presenting student work
Teaching Hints/Extensions—tips to explore and extend the topic and writing domain

In addition, at the end of each section is a reproducible rubric for evaluating student work. Give students the rubric at the beginning of the lesson so they can write with specific goals in mind.

The Writing Process

The writing process involves five steps: prewriting, writing a rough draft, revising, editing, and publishing/presenting the final product. These five steps are integral to any type of writing and form the foundation for the writing lessons in this book. Guide students through the stages of the process for each writing lesson, particularly the activities in the Independent Practice sections. Emphasize to students that they may need to repeat the cycle of revising and editing several times until their manuscript is ready for publication. Provide students with copies of the Writing Process Cards (page 13), and have them complete a card for each writing task and attach it to the final product. The first space for check-off in the Editing box of the Writing Process Card is for self-editing and the second is for peer or teacher editing.

Prewriting

Prewriting occurs after a thorough discussion of a topic but before formal writing about the topic. The prewriting stage is a structured brainstorming session aimed at eliciting spontaneous thinking about a specific topic. During the prewriting stage, help students use clusters and graphic organizers to organize their thoughts. For example, prewriting for a paragraph on gray whales might include a simple cluster such as the following:

The central idea, gray whales, becomes the basis for the topic sentence. The content of the cluster's spokes becomes the basis for supporting sentences.

A three-paragraph essay requires a cluster for each paragraph. The idea in the center of each cluster forms the basis for each topic sentence. The spokes contain the subjects for supporting sentences. The thesis statement for the entire essay is drawn from the three main points inside the circles. A possible thesis statement for an essay based on the following cluster is *My friendships include people from my school, my neighborhood, and my scout troop.*

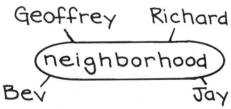

Other types of graphic organizers are helpful during the prewriting stage. The following example shows how to use another type of graphic organizer, a chart, to organize the previous topic. Throughout this book, you will find graphic organizers that help students organize their thinking and include the critical components in each of their writing products.

School	Neighborhood	Scouts
Lisa	Bev	Jo
Jan	Geoffrey	Sharon
Gail	Jay	Sammy
Dorothy	Richard	Jen
Rick		

FRIENDS

After students complete the brainstorming session, have them skim over their prewriting work and trim unnecessary or irrelevant content. The remaining information forms the skeleton or framework of the project.

Rough Draft

The rough draft is the first round of organized writing. During rough-draft writing, students write spontaneously, following the organizational framework of the prewriting graphic organizer. Students should feel free to deviate from the skeletal framework of the prewriting organizer, as long as the requirements of the writing type (as defined by the rubric) are met. Frequently, the most creative writing comes from the spontaneity of a rough draft.

Students should not worry about precise spelling and punctuation while writing rough drafts. During the editing stage, however, spelling and punctuation should be fine-tuned to perfection!

Revising

The revising stage requires students to reorganize at four levels: the entire piece, each paragraph (or stanza), each sentence (or line), and each individual word. Encourage students to revise in this order to save time and, potentially, unnecessary

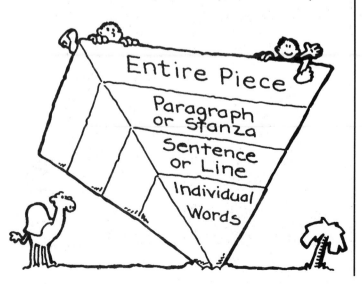

work. For example, if a writer deletes an entire paragraph, no time is wasted revising the sentences or words in that paragraph.

Revising the Entire Piece

At this level of revising, students look at the "big picture." They read and reread their writing, asking the following questions:

Does the piece flow from one idea to another?

Are paragraphs or stanzas in a logical sequence?

Are there transitions between paragraphs or stanzas?

Does the writing product meet the requirements of the rubric?

Is the writing clear and understandable?

Does the piece evoke emotion?

Does the piece contain sensory detail?

Could the content be rearranged to increase clarity?

Revising Each Paragraph or Stanza

In addition to larger organizational revising, students must revise their writing at the paragraph or stanza level. At this stage, students carefully examine each paragraph, asking the following:

For prose—

Are sentences arranged in a logical order?

Is there a topic sentence?

Are there supporting sentences?

Have I avoided redundancy?

Does each paragraph add to the clarity, depth, and/or intensity of the piece?

For poetry—

Does the main idea flow through each stanza?

Does the main emotion flow through each stanza?

Are lines effectively sequenced?

Does each stanza add to the clarity, depth, and/or intensity of the piece?

Writing Tip

It is common for beginning writers to struggle with the sentence order of a paragraph. Model the following "cut-and-paste" methods to demonstrate how to revise a paragraph.

1. Cut and paste using the computer.
2. Physically cut and paste the text to different sections of the page.
3. Color-code sentences that belong together.

Revising Each Sentence or Line

Students may wish to reorder or revise words within sentences (or lines) to strengthen the meaning conveyed to the reader as well as to add interest.

Weak Example:

I felt bad about the situation.

Strong Example:

My eyes swelled with tears over the situation.

Word efficiency is another aspect of sentence revision. Students should be taught to use as few as words as necessary to relay the desired meaning.

Weak Example:

The wood cabinet made of mahogany was beautiful, and we decided to buy it.

Strong example:

We decided to buy the beautiful mahogany cabinet.

Revising Individual Words

Revising word by word constitutes fine-tuning. This is the time to have students pull out the thesaurus and dictionary. This is the time to polish!

Here are some tips for revising at the word level:

Use interesting words—

> Weak Example:
> **The decorated shirt was pretty.**
>
> Strong Example:
> **The rhinestone-studded shirt dazzled everyone.**

Strengthen verbs—

> Weak Example:
> **She ate her dinner.**
>
> Strong Example:
> **She devoured her dinner.**

Clarify pronouns—

> Weak Example:
> **He met him at the park.**
>
> Strong Example:
> **Mr. Felig met Jonathan at the park.**

Clarify vague concepts—

> Weak Example:
> **Mr. Felig and Jonathan played a game.**
>
> Strong Example:
> **Mr. Felig and Jonathan played polo.**

Use sensory detail to evoke emotion—

> Weak Example:
> **She was sad.**
>
> Strong Example:
> **She couldn't hide her tear-stained cheeks and muffled sobs.**

Editing

At the editing stage, students make sure words are spelled correctly and punctuation is accurate. Here are some hints for this ongoing area of growth.

Editing Marks

Photocopy the Editing Marks reproducible (page 14) for students to refer to as they complete this stage of the writing process. Be sure students are familiar with and comfortable using editing symbols before they begin their first writing-process piece.

Spelling

Be sure students keep ongoing personal dictionaries in which they record new words they encounter. Included in these dictionaries should be a list of the most commonly used words in their writing. Also, be sure students have access to comprehensive dictionaries and thesauruses. Reinforce the idea that students may need to repeat the editing stage for any particular writing project.

If your students write using a computer, teach them how to use programs that check spelling. However, be sure that they clearly understand that computers will not detect missing words or homophone errors.

Punctuation

Mastering punctuation can be challenging. Teach punctuation as you teach writing, starting with the basics (ending punctuation and capitalization) and moving to commas, semicolons, and colons as students gain mastery. Do not expect perfection at the rough-draft stage. The goal of teaching writing is to help students improve their writing with each revision.

Repeated Reading

Students often have the misconception that one round of reading is sufficient in editing a piece. Encourage several reads by several people (the author, peers, and adults). Each reading provides an opportunity to improve the writing. For peer editing, students might engage in a round-robin discussion or an "author's chair," where one student reads a piece to the group or class and solicits constructive feedback.

Publishing/Presenting

The most rewarding aspect of the writing process is the final draft, or publishing/presenting stage. At this point, the writer finally sees his or her completed work in polished form, available for others' enjoyment. Provide forums for students to read their writing to one another, to other classes, and to parents. Encourage students to bind their writing into books and submit copies to school and classroom libraries. Students may also want to submit their work to local newspapers for publication. Tape-record stories for reading centers and post students' writing in your classroom on bulletin board displays.

Writing Devices

Certain literary devices can increase the effectiveness and beauty of students' writing. These devices include alliteration, metaphor, simile, sensory detail, onomatopoeia, and personification. Review these devices throughout your writing lessons, particularly during the revising stage. Challenge students to locate these devices in their independent reading materials.

Alliteration

Increase students' understanding of how alliteration—a string of words with the same initial sound—enhances the "sound" of language. Read and recite classic tongue twisters (*Peter Piper picked a peck of pickled peppers),* make up original tongue twisters (*Rhonda Rhino wrestled raggedy Rita Rhino),* and brainstorm phrases that include repetitive initial sounds (*Sally's savory sweets, Dominating Dominic,* and *Veronica Victor's venom).* Challenge students to complete these alliterative phrases and use alliteration in their writing. The use of alliteration is especially effective in poetry such as quatrains and limericks, where an author composes poetic phrases that evoke mental images and have auditory appeal because of the sound repetition.

Metaphor

Increase students' ability to relay meaning to a reader by comparing two ideas using "word pictures," or metaphors. Read some ordinary sentences and enhance the meaning of the sentences by rewriting them using metaphors.

Weak Example:
The manuscript has a lot of good qualities and can be improved.

Strong Example:
The manuscript is a diamond in the rough.

Weak Example:
The young man is very strong and one day will be in the Olympics.

Strong Example:
Such a young Hercules will one day compete in the Olympics.

Simile

Similar to metaphor, a simile compares two ideas using *as* or *like*. Help students enjoy similes by reading *Quick As a Cricket* by Audrey Wood. Discuss simile examples in the book, such as "quick as a cricket" and "strong as an ox." Discuss how similes evoke images that enhance the mental pictures of what the writer is trying to relate.

Sensory Detail

Writers who use sensory detail (words and phrases that vividly describe sight, sound, smell, taste, and touch) involve the reader's senses and add interest to their writing.

Weak Example:
I felt hot and tired after the race through the desert.

Strong Example:
Every inch of my body ached after the grueling race through the scorching, arid desert.

Onomatopoeia

Onomatopoeic words represent the sounds of the things they describe, for example, *crunch*, *crackle*, and *bang*. These words help clarify readers' mental images and intensify events and emotions.

Weak Example:
I heard a loud sound come from next door.

Strong Example:
Bang! The explosive sound pierced the air.

Weak Example:
The magician made the object disappear.

Strong Example:
Poof! With a swish of the magician's wand, the object disappeared.

Personification

Personification is the assigning of human characteristics to a nonhuman object. To provide students practice with this device, guide them in brainstorming a list of objects and the human characteristics that could describe them. Then, create sentences using items from this personification list. For example, students might use the word *shy* to describe the moon. Then, they might write the sentence *The moon shyly peeked through the clouds.*

Assessment

Each lesson in this resource includes a rubric for evaluating student work. These rubrics allow readers to assess the critical components, style issues, originality, and mechanics of the work. They also include space for readers' comments.

Rubrics are valuable tools at all stages of the writing process. Give the rubrics to students as they begin prewriting to help them understand the criteria by which their work will be assessed. At this early stage, rubrics also help students understand the focus and purpose of each writing genre.

As students revise their own work, rubrics help them assess the quality of what they have written. Have students complete a rubric for each draft they write and include detailed comments each time. Also, have peer editors complete rubrics when evaluating classmates' work. Objectively evaluating one's own work is a difficult task, to be sure. Give students practice evaluating each other's work. When students make tactful, constructive comments, they contribute to the improvement of each other's writing.

Rubrics also give you a standardized format for the final assessment of students' writing. Ask students to attach all of their completed rubrics to each project they turn in. Use the student-completed rubrics to assess the progress students made while writing.

When you complete the final rubric and present it to students, they will clearly understand why they received the grades they were given.

As students complete writing projects, you may want to store their work in portfolios. Whether your portfolios are simple file folders in a file cabinet or decorated pizza boxes in which students can store artwork that accompanies their writing, be sure students have open access to them. Invite students to add at any time work they feel shows growth or excellence. Review these portfolios when determining students' writing grades, and have them available for parents to look through at Open House and at parent-teacher conferences.

Writing Process Cards

Prewriting	Rough draft	Revising	Editing	Publishing

Directions: Check or initial each stage as you complete it. Attach a completed card to your final draft. Attach your previous work (prewriting, rough draft, revising, and editing pages) behind your final draft to show the stages of your writing process.

Prewriting	Rough draft	Revising	Editing	Publishing

Directions: Check or initial each stage as you complete it. Attach a completed card to your final draft. Attach your previous work (prewriting, rough draft, revising, and editing pages) behind your final draft to show the stages of your writing process.

Prewriting	Rough draft	Revising	Editing	Publishing

Directions: Check or initial each stage as you complete it. Attach a completed card to your final draft. Attach your previous work (prewriting, rough draft, revising, and editing pages) behind your final draft to show the stages of your writing process.

Prewriting	Rough draft	Revising	Editing	Publishing

Directions: Check or initial each stage as you complete it. Attach a completed card to your final draft. Attach your previous work (prewriting, rough draft, revising, and editing pages) behind your final draft to show the stages of your writing process.

Editing Marks

Editing Mark	Examples in Text	Meaning
≡	watch out!	Capitalize the letter.
/	Come here Quickly.	Use lowercase.
∧	Look at that girafe.	Insert a letter. (This symbol is called a caret.)
⊙	Place a period here ⊙	Insert a period.
∧	When it rains the geraniums love it.	Insert a comma.
¶	. . . with me. The next day . . .	Start a new paragraph.
⌄ ⌄	"Good morning, Sally called.	Insert quotations.
⌣	pop corn	Join words.
ℓ	June and and Deborah wrote this book.	Delete this word.
∧	Luella Carolea like it. *and*	Insert a word.
∽	Can you with come me?	Reverse word order.
#	Make a wise decision.	Insert a space.

Expressive Writing © 1998 Creative Teaching Press

Caption

Critical Components

A caption expresses the mood or emotion of a drawing or photograph. A caption expresses the content of a drawing or photograph. Captions are brief—usually one to three sentences.

Preparation

Gather uncaptioned inspiring scenic or action photographs from old calendars and travel magazines. Make an overhead transparency of page 18. Photocopy pages 19 and 20 for students. Have students cut out captioned scenic and action photographs from old calendars and travel magazines, or locate them in books.

Setting the Stage

Ask students to share their photographs. Ask a few students to read aloud the captions published with these scenes. Explain that the role of a caption is to capture the mood, emotion, and content of a picture. Explain that caption writing is an important part of many people's jobs, including book writers and journalists.

Instructional Input

1. Write the following caption on an overhead projector or chalkboard.

The tranquil village, blanketed in white, reflects the peaceful aftermath of a storm. Clear skies and bright sunshine begin to melt the snow, revealing the leafless branches of surrounding forests.

2. Ask students to identify the words that capture the content (*village, clear skies, sunshine, snow, leafless branches, forests*) and the mood (*tranquil, peaceful aftermath, bright sunshine*) of a photograph that might accompany this caption.

3. Place these words in a two-column chart to help students see how a caption's vocabulary captures the mood and content of the captioned image.

4. Review the critical components of a caption: words that capture mood, words that capture content, and brevity.

5. Show how the revising stage of the writing process can move a caption from a weak draft to average to strong. Use the following examples, or write weak, average, and strong captions to accompany a photograph or poster that you have displayed.

Example 1

Weak:

The little town is covered in snow. The trees have no leaves.

Average:

The storm is over and the village is blanketed with snow. There are clear skies and leafless trees.

Strong:

The tranquil village, blanketed in white, reflects the peaceful aftermath of a storm. Clear skies and bright sunshine begin to melt the snow, revealing the leafless branches of surrounding forests.

Example 2

Weak:

Here is a green valley with a creek. You can see the little house and the wood bridge.

Average:

The V-shaped valley has a creek running through it. A lone cabin and bridge show that someone lives there.

Strong:

Nestled in the crevice of a glacial valley, the isolated cabin offers shelter to a weary traveler. The lone wood bridge provides safe passage over the rapid river.

Guided Practice

1. Show students the overhead transparency of page 18.

2. Discuss with students how strong verbs, precise nouns, and vivid adjectives increase the effectiveness of these captions. As a class, create a two-column chart similar to the one from the Instructional Input section for each strong example.

3. Evaluate the examples as a class, using the Caption Rubric on page 20 to examine whether the words captured the mood and content of the picture.

4. Display two or three large color photos. Walk the class through the first stages of the writing process as you create a caption for each photo. Guide students in revising the captions to make them stronger.

Independent Practice

1. Give each student a copy of page 19.

2. Read aloud the sample caption and then invite students to choose several photographs and write captions independently. Have them follow the steps of the writing process as they write, revise, and edit their work.

Presentation

- Conduct a "write-around-the-room." Invite each student to choose a photograph, write a caption about it, and staple the photograph and caption together. On the command *Pass,* have students pass their papers to a classmate. Instruct students to edit their neighbor's work and offer revising suggestions. Have them pass the papers every two minutes until they have made suggestions on several students' papers. This peer feedback helps raise the quality of writing prior to students submitting it to you.

- Create a classroom newspaper containing photographs of day-to-day classroom activities and student-written captions. Make the newspaper available at Back-to-School Night or Open House.

- Post photographs and captions on a bulletin board titled *Colorful Captions.*

Teaching Hints/Extensions

- Conduct exercises that help students add sensory detail to improve their captions. Sports photographs work well here. A sample caption with sensory detail might read *Beads of perspiration trickled down his forehead. The overhead sun glared down, but his concentration would not be broken. His stride grew longer and the race was won.*

- Encourage students to create family photo albums that include student-written captions with photographs of family trips or events.

- Use photography to record field trips. Invite students to write captions for the photographs and compile them into class albums.

Caption Samples

Example One

Weak:
There is a building in the valley.

Average:
The deep valley conceals an old stone church.

Strong:
The abandoned stone church, shrouded in fog, lies concealed in a valley of fall colors.

Example Two

Weak:
The big city has a river outside it.

Average:
Beneath the blue sky, the large buildings look out onto a river and brush.

Strong:
A clear blue sky, a swiftly running river, and green trees and shrubs surround the large desolate city.

Expressive Writing © 1998 Creative Teaching Press

Name:_____

Writing Captions

Directions: Examine the two-column chart for the caption below. This chart is a record of words that capture the content and mood of the picture. Then choose three photographs. Brainstorm your ideas in a two-column chart first, and then write your caption on the lines next to your chart. Evaluate each caption against the Caption Rubric and revise. Attach the photographs to your finished work.

The peaceful river follows its ancient course as the city awakens to the breathtaking music of the cathedral bells. The rich forest-green bushes and trees surrounding the city glitter in the golden showers of morning sunlight.
— Student Author: Katie Holder

mood	content
peaceful	city
ancient	cathedral bells
breathtaking	bushes
music	trees
golden showers	sunlight
of morning	
sunlight	

Caption One:

mood	content

_____

_____

_____

_____

Caption Two:

mood	content

_____

_____

_____

_____

Caption Three:

mood	content

_____

_____

_____

_____

Expressive Writing © 1998 Creative Teaching Press

Writer's Name: _____   Evaluator's Name: _____

Caption Rubric

	Great!	O.K.	Needs Help
Critical Components			
Expresses the emotion of the drawing or photograph			
Expresses the content of the drawing or photograph			
Brief—one to three sentences			
Style			
Strong, active verbs			
Precise words			
Words that evoke images and express sensory detail			
Writing devices such as alliteration, metaphor, simile, onomatopoeia, and personification			
Originality			
Mechanics			
Ending punctuation			
Capitalization			
Comma rules			
Quotation marks			

Comments

_____

_____

_____

_____

Expressive Writing © 1998 Creative Teaching Press

Dialogue

Critical Components

A dialogue records the exact words spoken between two or more characters. A dialogue uses verbs and adjectives that vividly express tone and emotion. A dialogue includes

- a new paragraph each time a different person talks.

- indented paragraphs.

- quotation marks around spoken words.

- ending punctuation inside quotation marks.

- vivid verbs that capture emotion, such as *chuckled, fretted,* or *announced*

Preparation

Gather fun comic strips that include clear examples of dialogue (at least one per student). Make an overhead transparency of each comic strip. Make an overhead transparency of page 24. Photocopy pages 25–27 for students. Have students bring copies of favorite comic strips.

Setting the Stage

Invite students to share their comic strips in small groups or pairs. Give students the comic strips you gathered. Project the transparencies on the overhead projector and read the strips as a class. Introduce the concept of "dialogue" in the context of the comic strips.

Instructional Input

1. Define dialogue for students as a situation in which characters are talking to each other.

2. Discuss how some comic strips are forms of dialogue, and cite examples from your comic-strip transparencies.

3. Rewrite one of the comic strips into a dialogue and project it on an overhead projector. As you write the dialogue, model the critical components, style, and mechanics listed on the Dialogue Rubric on page 27.

4. Ask students the following questions.

How are the comic strip and the formal dialogue similar? (They have the same verbal text.)

How are they different? (The formal dialogue includes quotation marks, ending punctuation, paragraphs, and verbs and adjectives that express the tone of the spoken words.)

How do you know where to place the quotation marks in the formal dialogue? (Quotation marks are always placed around the words the person says.)

What is the purpose of including in a formal dialogue vivid verbs, such as wailed, whispered, *or* wondered? (These verbs more accurately capture the emotion of the dialogue and enhance the reader's mental image of the text.)

Guided Practice

1. Show students the overhead transparency of page 24—a dialogue titled *Mrs. Peterson and the Pet Store.* Ask them to identify words spoken by each character.

2. Underline what Mrs. Peterson says using a red overhead pen and what Lauren says using a blue overhead pen to identify each character's words. Discuss the critical components of dialogue within the context of this example.

3. Remove the transparency from the overhead projector. Distribute copies of page 25 and ask students to insert quotation marks where they are needed.

4. Show again the overhead transparency of page 24 so students can check their papers.

5. Provide each student with a copy of the Dialogue Rubric on page 27. Invite students to use the rubric to evaluate *Mrs. Peterson and the Pet Store,* and have them check carefully for the critical components.

Independent Practice

1. Brainstorm as a class a list of famous inventors, scientists, presidents, social activists, religious leaders, artists, musicians, athletes, writers, and explorers about whom students may wish to write.

2. Have students write a dialogue between themselves and a person from the list.

Encourage them to use words that vividly capture the emotions they might feel during this conversation. Invite students to research the information for accuracy. (This step includes practice in both the expressive and informative writing domains.)

Presentation

- Encourage students to create illustrations of the characters in their dialogues. Post dialogues with the illustrations on a bulletin board titled *Conversations with Famous Faces.*

- Have students select partners. Invite partners to rehearse and perform each other's dialogue in a short-play form.

Teaching Hints/Extensions

- Erase or cover the text from several comic strips. Give students copies of the strips and challenge them to fill in the dialogue. (You may want to laminate the strips to make them reusable.)

- Encourage formal dialogue practice by having students "translate" their favorite comics into formal dialogues.

- Invite each student to illustrate in comic-strip form a favorite scene from a book or story. Ask students to include dialogues written in speech bubbles to go with each scene in their comic strip.

- Hold a "Dialogue Hunt." Have students search through literature to find the funniest, scariest, most curious, or most unusual dialogues to share with the class during an oral discussion. Post students' findings on a bulletin board display.

- Encourage students to begin stories with dialogues that grab the reader's attention right from the start. For example, a story might begin *Shhhh, I think I hear someone coming!*

- Use the Dialogue Verbs Word Bank on page 26 as a student resource sheet. Encourage students to add to this word bank whenever they find a new dialogue verb. Have them store their word banks in their writing folders. Create a chart-size version of the word bank to display and add to over time.

Dialogue Sample

• Mrs. Peterson and the Pet Store •
Student Author: Lauren Miller

"Hello, Mrs. Peterson," I said cheerfully.

"Well, hello Lauren," Mrs. Peterson responded. "What kind of pet would you like to see on this fine afternoon?"

"I think I would like to see some kittens," I announced.

"Good choice. Here are the kittens," Mrs. Peterson replied.

I went to the cage. There were so many kittens, and they were all so cute. Then, I spotted the cutest one of all.

"Oh, Mrs. Peterson! Look at the kitten with the gray fur, and look at its tiny paws with white socks. I like its pink nose!" I exclaimed. "Don't you?"

"Yes, Lauren. He is very cute. Would you like to buy him?" Mrs. Peterson inquired.

"I certainly would like to buy him. How much does he cost?" I wondered aloud.

"He costs $75.00," Mrs. Peterson answered.

"Great!" I announced happily.

Expressive Writing © 1998 Creative Teaching Press

Using Quotation Marks

Directions: Read the dialogue and insert quotations marks where appropriate.

(Hint: There are eleven missing sets of quotation marks.)

• Mrs. Peterson and the Pet Store •

Student Author: Lauren Miller

Hello Mrs. Peterson, I said cheerfully.

Well, hello Lauren, Mrs. Peterson responded. What kind of pet would you like to see on this fine afternoon?

I think I would like to see some kittens, I announced.

Good choice. Here are the kittens, Mrs. Peterson replied.

I went to the cage. There were so many kittens, and they were all so cute. Then, I spotted the cutest one of all.

Oh, Mrs. Peterson! Look at the kitten with the gray fur, and look at its tiny paws with white socks. I like its pink nose, I exclaimed. Don't you?

Yes, Lauren. He is very cute. Would you like to buy him? Mrs. Peterson inquired.

I certainly would like to buy him. How much does he cost? I wondered aloud.

He costs $75.00, Mrs. Peterson answered.

Great! I announced happily.

Discussion

1. Do you think Lauren had enough money to buy the kitten? Which words are your clue?

2. Describe Lauren's emotions during her visit to the pet store. Which words vividly express these emotions?

Name:_____

Dialogue Verbs Word Bank

admitted	interrupted	
announced	jested	
argued	joked	
bragged	kidded	
cautioned	laughed	
coaxed	ordered	
confessed	praised	
declared	pried	
demanded	promised	
exhorted	queried	
expounded	sang	
expressed	snickered	
extolled	spewed	
hollered	stammered	
inserted	stuttered	
insisted	suggested	
insulted	whispered	

Expressive Writing © 1998 Creative Teaching Press

Writer's Name: _____ Evaluator's Name: _____

Dialogue Rubric

	Great!	O.K.	Needs Help
Critical Components			
Uses verbs and adjectives to vividly express tone and emotion			
Changes paragraphs each time a new person talks			
Indents each paragraph			
Uses quotation marks around spoken words			
Places ending punctuation inside quotation marks			
Style			
Strong, active verbs			
Precise words			
Words that evoke images and express sensory detail			
Writing devices such as alliteration, metaphor, simile, onomatopoeia, and personification			
Originality			
Mechanics			
Ending punctuation			
Capitalization			
Comma rules			
Quotation marks			
Paragraph structure			

Comments

_____

_____

_____

_____

Journal

Critical Components

A journal is a record of personal events, describing the writer's feelings, thoughts, and observations. Journal entries are written in chronological order and dated. A journal entry is written with the author as the only intended audience. A journal provides a private way to express feelings and emotions, allows for daydreaming and planning, and helps its author remember important events.

Preparation

Bring to class as many examples of journals and diaries as possible. (Refer to the bibliography section for a list of recommended published diaries.) If you kept a journal as a child, or if you currently keep one, select an appropriate entry to share with the class. Make overhead transparencies of pages 31 and 32. Photocopy pages 32 and 33 for students.

Setting the Stage

Ask students to name people they know that keep or have kept a diary or journal. Invite students that keep diaries or journals to describe the benefits of them.

Instructional Input

1. Share one or more entries from a private or published journal. Explain to students that much that we know about historical figures was learned from their diaries or journals, and that biographers and auto-biographers use diaries and journals for gathering and organizing subject matter.

2. Brainstorm with students the types of information that are often recorded in journals. Chart responses on chart paper or the chalkboard.

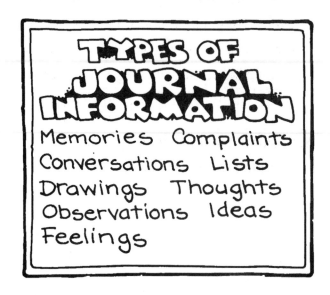

TYPES OF JOURNAL INFORMATION

Memories   Complaints
Conversations   Lists
Drawings   Thoughts
Observations   Ideas
Feelings

3. Encourage students to begin (or continue with) a private at-home journal to help them express and understand their experiences and feelings.

4. Display the overhead transparency of the Journal Frame on page 32. Explain that this page emphasizes elements included in a journal entry—a description of a specific experience and reflective thoughts, feelings, and observations.

5. Choose a shared school experience (e.g., field trip, assembly, guest speaker) or a shared community experience (e.g., storm, earthquake, parade) with which all students are familiar. Complete the journal frame as a group, listing feelings, thoughts, and observations that this experience generated.

Guided Practice

1. Show students the overhead transparency of the Journal Sample on page 31. Read and discuss the entry with the class.

2. Have students summarize the described event. Then, circle phrases that describe the author's observations, thoughts, and feelings about the event. Use a different color overhead pen for each category.

3. Evaluate the journal entry using the Journal Rubric on page 33.

Independent Practice

1. To assist students in brainstorming and prewriting the content of their journal entry, provide them with copies of the Journal Frame on page 32.

2. Invite students to write a journal entry about a special school event such as a party, trip, or holiday; a personal victory such as winning a race or learning a new skill; or a difficult situation such as a fight with a friend or starting a new school. Remind students to omit anything they do not wish to be read by others.

3. Have students write journal entries detailing the days leading up to and following their first entry. Invite them to describe the anticipation and aftermath of the main event.

Presentation

- Since the nature of diary writing is private, students may not be comfortable having their assignment published. Instead, they may want to self-evaluate using the rubric on page 33, or meet privately with the teacher to gain input and discuss the rubric together. They may also share their entry with a trusted classmate.

- Invite students to tape-record themselves reading their journal entries. If they are keeping at-home journals, invite them to keep a tape-recorded version as well as their written version.

Teaching Hints/Extensions

- Students often enjoy writing journal entries from the perspective of a fictional character or the creator of a fictional character. Have students choose a character from or author of a favorite book. They should then select an event in that person or character's life and write a journal entry from the perspective of their chosen character. The following excerpt was written after a student read a biography of Jules Verne.

- Encourage students to ask older family members about their childhood memories. Have students record the family members' stories in a diary or journal to be passed on to future generations.

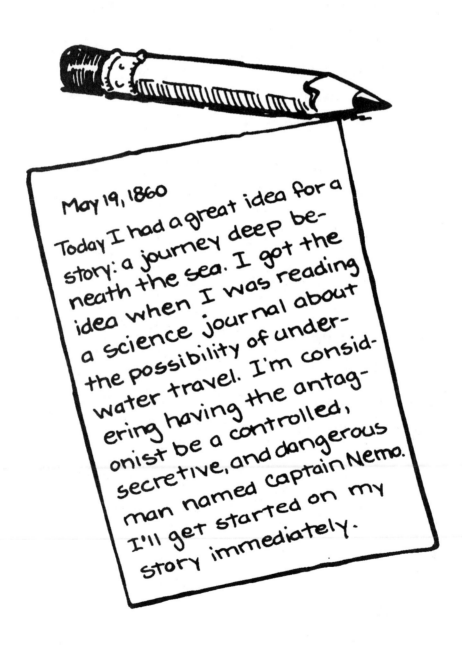

May 19, 1860
Today I had a great idea for a story: a journey deep beneath the sea. I got the idea when I was reading a science journal about the possibility of underwater travel. I'm considering having the antagonist be a controlled, secretive, and dangerous man named Captain Nemo. I'll get started on my story immediately.

Journal Sample

December 25

Dear Journal,

Today is Christmas. I woke up early because a puppy was licking my face. My mom and dad and my brothers were telling me to wake up while the puppy was licking me. When I finally woke up, I realized the puppy was the same one I played with at the pet shop the week before. I was so excited I thought I would burst!

She is a pretty dog. She has yellow fur and her stomach is pink and white. Whenever she scratches herself, all of the skin around her neck completely buries her face. Every time my little brother Brett talks about her, he calls her "the dog with the little brown nose."

The hardest thing I had to do today was find the right name for her. I wanted her name to fit her just right. Tonight when we were eating dinner, we told her to stay in the kitchen and she listened to what we said. After dinner, I decided to name her Angel because she behaved like one.

It will be hard for me to go to sleep tonight because I am so happy. I love her so much, I want to stay up and play with her. Angel is the best Christmas gift I ever received!

Sincerely,

Evan Lee

Name:_____

Journal Frame

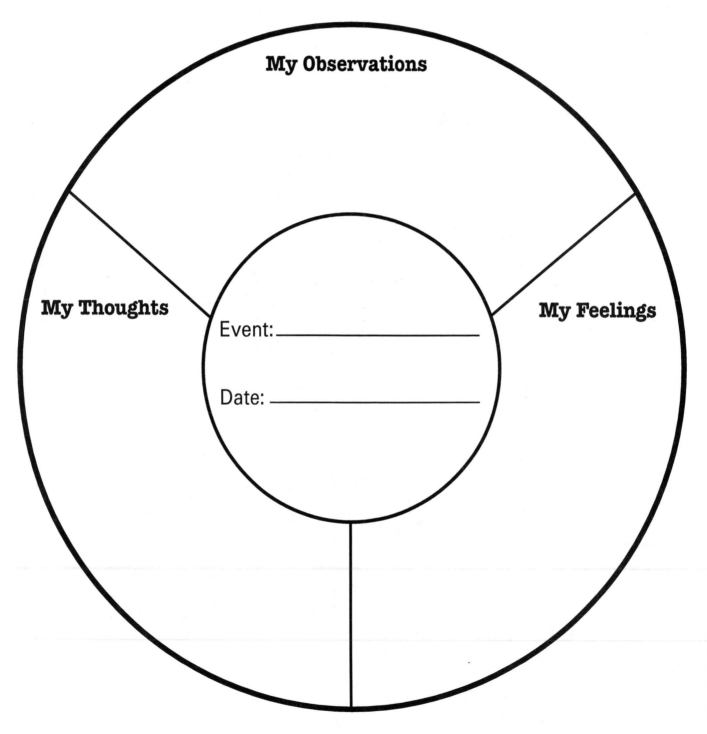

My Observations

My Thoughts

Event:_____

Date:_____

My Feelings

Expressive Writing © 1998 Creative Teaching Press

Writer's Name: _____   Evaluator's Name: _____

Journal Rubric

	Great!	O.K.	Needs Help
Critical Components			
Details the recollection of a personal experience			
Entries are dated and written in chronological order			
Contains the writer's feelings, thoughts, and observations			
Style			
Strong, active verbs			
Precise words			
Words that evoke images and express sensory detail			
Writing devices such as alliteration, metaphor, simile, onomatopoeia, and personification			
Originality			
Mechanics			
Ending punctuation			
Capitalization			
Comma rules			
Quotation marks			
Paragraph structure			

Comments

_____

_____

_____

_____

Expressive Writing © 1998 Creative Teaching Press

Character Sketch

Critical Components

Character sketches describe qualities, experiences, or viewpoints of a person or character. Character sketches may include descriptions of the character's

- early life
- growing-up years
- important relationships
- important events
- personal beliefs
- major accomplishments
- contributions to society

Preparation

Write a short sketch about yourself that includes the critical components listed above. Prepare and post cards that state the critical components of a character sketch. Make an overhead transparency of page 36. Photocopy pages 37–39 for students.

Character Sketches
Qualities, Experiences, Viewpoints
Early Life
Growing-Up Years
Important Relationships
Important Events
Personal Beliefs
Major Accomplishments
Contributions to Society

Setting the Stage

Read aloud the character sketch about yourself. Invite students to ask questions or make comments about your sketch.

Instructional Input

1. Point out on the posted cards the critical components of a character sketch.

2. Check for student comprehension of your character sketch by asking students at least one question about each critical component.

Guided Practice

1. Show students the overhead transparency of the student-authored sample on page 36.

2. Ask students to read this character sketch with you and respond to the following questions:

What does this character sketch tell you about the author's growing-up years?

What factor(s) limits the length of this character sketch and prevents the author from describing her major accomplishments?

What does this sketch tell you about the author's personality?

3. Distribute to students copies of pages 37 and 38. Have them read the character sketch about the author's grandmother and answer the discussion questions at the end of page 38. If students need additional reinforcement about the critical components of a character sketch, ask them to color-code the critical components as they read the passage.

Independent Practice

1. Have students brainstorm the critical components they would like to include in their own character sketch before writing their rough draft.

2. Invite students to write a sketch about themselves, or a family member, friend, or famous person.

Presentation

- Invite students to use the Character Sketch Rubric on page 39 to give peer feedback. Encourage students to give helpful hints to one another, encouraging anecdotes that provide glimpses or "snapshots" of their character's personality.

Teaching Hints/Extensions

- Integrate the assignment into the period of history you are studying. Ask each student to write a character sketch about a personality that lived during that time period. Invite students to dress in appropriate costumes as they read their sketches. Bind the finished works in books with titles such as *Voices of American History* or *Voices of Ancient Greece.*

- Invite students to choose a character sketch from *Lives of the Writers, Lives of the Musicians,* or *Lives of the Artists* by Kathleen Krull and Kathryn Hewitt and read or perform the character sketch as a monologue.

- Use character sketches to explore in cooperative groups family relationships, historical figures, and point of view. For example, one group might write sketches about Martin Luther King, Jr., from the perspective of his wife, children, or parents. Then, to give the class various perspectives from the same family, have the groups perform their sketches.

- Invite students to explore first person and third person by having them write and perform the same character sketch in both voices.

Character Sketch
Sample 1

• A Story about ME! •
Student Author: Maribeth Johnson

I was born on a sunny spring day in Fort Thomas, Kentucky, March 18, 1987. My sisters, Brooke and Shaina, were there watching me being born. My dad was holding my mom's hand.

In the summertime, I would go to our neighborhood pool and to Highland Park with my mom. In the wintertime, my family and I would go Christmas caroling. When we got back, we had bonfires and drank hot chocolate.

When I was five, I got a new bike for my birthday. My best friend, Julie, wanted to ride it. I am a very generous person, but I could not let her ride my shiny bike that day.

The Christmas that I was five years old, my dad became an FBI agent. My family was transferred to Saginaw, Michigan. At our apartment, my dad taught me how to ride a two-wheeler. If I rode a certain number of feet, I would get a treat.

A couple of years after we moved to our new house, my mom got a cat named Basil. One Christmas, my family and I went ice fishing. Basil liked fish, but it was too cold for him to go.

Then my family volunteered to transfer to California. My dad and I traveled through nine different states on the way to our new house. My mom and sisters flew on a plane to meet us here. I even got to see the Grand Canyon. Now I have lived in California for one year, and it is the best year ever!

Expressive Writing © 1998 Creative Teaching Press

Character Sketch
Sample 2

• Dena Marie Neyenesch •

Student Author: Tess Vreeland

Although Dena Marie was born on September 6, 1933, in Bethlehem, Pennsylvania, to Harry and Alberta Neyenesch, if you ask her about her date and place of birth, she'll tell you "I was born on Earth, when my mother delivered me."

All her life, Dena Marie Neyenesch has been changing—changing homes, changing schools, changing careers, changing pets, changing friends, and even changing her name.

While growing up, Dena moved all over southeastern Pennsylvania, and one of the things she remembers most is walking to school everywhere she lived. She told me that in one town she took the shortcut "over the river and through the woods" and does not remember a time she ever fell in the river. "That doesn't mean I never fell in. It just means I don't remember a time when I did," she told me.

When Dena was in fifth grade, she was diagnosed with scarlet fever, but strangely enough, it only lasted one day. Still, her mother, two sisters, and brother were quarantined in the house with her for 30 days. Dena's father was allowed to go to work. He was the only one who could go out of the house. Dena was confined to her room the entire time and would play with paper dolls through the crack under the door with her sister, Carol.

Dena loved games and sports and joined as many girls' teams as she could find, but trust me, girls' teams were not very common. When Dena became an adult, she even said she wanted to have nine children just so she could have her own baseball team.

When Dena was 19 years old, she married Alden Kelley. They had six children—Kris, Kevin, Kim, Kendall, Kerri, and Karli. After 21 years, they got divorced, and Dena married a man named Bill Chapman and had another son, Kamaran. They were married about ten years and after they got divorced, she changed her name back to Kelley, because she said she had been a Kelley longer than she had been anything else in her life—and, besides, it would be easier to remember. As long as we're talking about kids, Dena now has 18 grandchildren and one great-grandchild. Wow!

As far as jobs go, Dena has done them all. She has been a waitress, a librarian, a drugstore cashier, a carhop, a foster mother, a kindergarten teacher, a baby-sitter, a toy-store clerk, a fish-counter attendant, a big-rig driver, a construction foreman, a parts runner, and a registered nurse. She says her least favorite job was teaching kindergarten because the kids were smarter than she was. What she has always most wanted professionally was to be retired, and her favorite job was always the next one.

Dena moved a lot as a child and still moves around a lot today. She enjoys traveling and camping as much as she can, whether it's a quick weekend trip to the desert or the mountains or a cross-country, monthlong sightseeing trip with the family. Just ask—she's ready to go!

I think Dena's most important characteristic is her humor, which she shares with everyone, and I should know . . . she's my grandma!

Discussion

1. What words does the author use to effectively describe her grandmother's early years?

_____

_____

2. Describe how the author illustrates her grandmother's contributions to society.

_____

_____

3. Analyze Dena Marie Neyenesch's life. What kind of personality does she have? What evidence in the character sketch gives you clues?

_____

_____

Expressive Writing © 1998 Creative Teaching Press

Writer's Name: _____   Evaluator's Name: _____

Character Sketch Rubric

	Great!	O.K.	Needs Help
Critical Components			
Describes the qualities, experiences, or viewpoints of a person or character			
Includes information regarding the character's			
early life			
growing-up years			
important relationships			
important events			
personal beliefs			
major accomplishments			
contributions to society			
Style			
Strong, active verbs			
Precise words			
Words that evoke images and express sensory detail			
Writing devices such as alliteration, metaphor, simile, onomatopoeia, and personification			
Originality			
Mechanics			
Ending punctuation			
Capitalization			
Comma rules			
Quotation marks			
Paragraph structure			

Comments

_____

_____

Expressive Writing © 1998 Creative Teaching Press

Quatrain

Critical Components

A quatrain is a four-line poem in which each line has a strong rhythm and similar syllable count. A quatrain can be written about any subject and can be silly or serious. A quatrain does not need to rhyme, but it can have a variety of rhyming patterns, such as AAAA, ABAB, ABCB, and AABB.

Preparation

Locate several quatrains, serious and silly, to read to students. Make an overhead transparency of page 43. Photocopy pages 44 and 45 for students. Have students bring in poetry books from home and select a favorite quatrain to share with the class.

Setting the Stage

Begin by reading several quatrains to the class. These should range from serious to silly and include several different rhyming patterns. Divide the class into small groups and have students share their chosen quatrain with the group and explain why it is their favorite. Have each group vote on one favorite quatrain. Record these poems on chart paper.

Instructional Input

1. Explain to students that the letters A, B, C, and D are used to help identify rhyming patterns. Rhyming patterns in quatrains are determined by the last word of each line. If two or more lines rhyme, they are assigned the same letter. Share with students the example on page 44.

> **Rain**
> by Amanda Cech
>
> Making plants grow strong and tall,
> Cold and wet, the rain does fall.
> Full of life, so crisp and clear,
> Rain's soft sound I long to hear.

2. Have students practice creating rhyming couplets (two-line rhyming poems) before you introduce writing quatrains.

3. As a class, examine the rhyming pattern and syllable count of each group's favorite quatrain. Appoint a recorder to write the appropriate rhyming pattern next to each poem on the chart paper.

4. Have students conduct a quatrain search, looking in their own books and those you provide for quatrains that match the rhyming pattern of poems on the chart paper. Invite students to read these aloud for everyone to enjoy.

Guided Practice

1. Display the overhead transparency of the quatrain samples on page 43.

2. Read each poem aloud and have students use hand signals or individual chalkboards to identify the rhyming pattern and syllable count.

3. Write one or more quatrains as a class, modeling the process of choosing a topic and a rhyming pattern and brainstorming possible rhyming words. Demonstrate to students how to use a rhyming dictionary.

Independent Practice

1. Provide each student with a copy of the Quatrain Frame on page 44.

2. Have each student write one or more quatrains using his or her favorite rhyming pattern(s). You may wish to focus students on a specific topic or subject matter.

3. Once students have an understanding of the basic quatrain format, invite them to practice their skills by having them write a specialized quatrain, such as a clerihew or opposite poem. (See Teaching Hints/Extensions for explanations of these poetry styles.)

Presentation

- Organize students' completed quatrains into categories, such as humorous poems, nature poems, or poems about pets. Bind collections of poems together by theme and keep them in your class library.

- Practice expressive reading and presentation of poetry. Encourage students to memorize their poems and focus on the clarity and pace necessary for public speaking.

Teaching Hints/Extensions

- A clerihew is a quatrain poem that pokes gentle fun at a celebrity or character, has an AABB rhyme pattern, and uses the following format:

  Line 1: ends with a person's name
  Line 2: rhymes with the name of the person in line one
  Lines 3 and 4: tell more about the person and rhyme with each other

- Read the clerihew titled "Goldilocks" to students, and have them write original clerihews about characters or celebrities.

- After reading the delightful poetry book *Opposites* by Richard Wilbur, invite students to work with partners to create opposite quatrains that begin with the first line *What is the opposite of _____?* The remaining three lines of the poem answer the question. A sample opposite poem is

  What is the opposite of fat?
  A hat upon which you have sat,
  A scrawny little baby bunny,
  A buzzing bee without his honey.

- Invite students to form groups and create scavenger hunts in which the clues are riddles written in quatrain form.

GOLDILOCKS

There is a young girl named Goldilocks,
Who goes into houses but never knocks.
She'll eat all your food and sit in your chair,
And when you get home, you'll give her a scare.

Quatrain Samples

• A Poem •
Student Author: Rachel Cech

A poem starts in the back of your head,
And you don't even know it's there.
It works its way to the front of your brain,
And seems to pop out of thin air!

A poem with people and places and things,
That tells about joy and despair.
That poem started in the back of your head,
And you didn't know it was there!

• Your Mind Is a Window •
Student Author: Rachel Cech

Your mind is a window deep within.
Your mind is a window taking things in.
Your mind is a window ready to grow,
Stretching to hold everything you know.

• Hair •
Student Author: Rachel Cech

Long hair, short, or in between,
When you swim, the ends turn green.
Take a handful, pull it out.
If you do I'll really shout!

• The Deer •
Student Author: Kelly Russell

The deer, the deer, so quick and fast,
Who jumps with so much grace.
When you see him, you will gasp
As you observe his pace.

• My Doll •
Student Author: Amanda Cech

I have a pretty doll,
And she is rather small.
Though I am fairly tall,
She doesn't mind at all.

Name:_____

Quatrain Frame

A quatrain is a poem written in four lines. Each line has a similar rhythm and syllable count.

A quatrain can be written about any subject and can be silly or serious.

A quatrain does not need to rhyme, but if it does, it can have a variety of rhyming patterns, such as AAAA, ABAB, ABCB, and AABB.

Example:

• Rain •

Student Author: Amanda Cech

Making plants grow strong and tall, (A)
Cold and wet the rain does fall. (A)
Full of life so crisp and clear, (B)
Rain's soft sound I love to hear. (B)

Write your own quatrains using a different rhyming pattern each time.

Expressive Writing © 1998 Creative Teaching Press

Quatrain Rubric

	Great!	O.K.	Needs Help
Critical Components			
Composed of four lines			
Each line has a strong rhythm and similar syllable count			
Follows a consistent rhyme pattern			
Style			
Strong, active verbs			
Precise words			
Words that evoke images and express sensory detail			
Writing devices such as alliteration, metaphor, simile, onomatopoeia, and personification			
Originality			
Mechanics			
Ending punctuation			
Capitalization			
Comma rules			
Quotation marks			

Comments

_____

_____

_____

_____

Limerick

Critical Components

A limerick is a light, humorous verse composed of five lines. A limerick contains three eight-syllable lines that rhyme and two five-syllables lines that rhyme (although the syllable count can vary to make the poem read smoothly). The format is as follows:

Line 1: rhyme pattern A (8 syllables)
Line 2: rhyme pattern A (8 syllables)
Line 3: rhyme pattern B (5 syllables)
Line 4: rhyme pattern B (5 syllables)
Line 5: rhyme pattern A (8 syllables)

Preparation

Bring to class samples of humorous limerick poetry, such as *The Book of Nonsense* by Edward Leer or *The Book of Pigericks* by Arnold Lobel. Make an overhead transparency of page 49. Photocopy pages 50 and 51 for students. Have students select a short humorous poem (preferably, a limerick) to share with classmates.

Setting the Stage

Have students read aloud their chosen poems. Allow time for discussion and exploration as students share what they enjoyed about the poems. Continue the discussion by reading aloud several limericks. Explain to students that the letters A, B, C, and D are used to help identify rhyming patterns. Rhyming patterns are determined by the last word in each line. If two or more lines rhyme, they are assigned the same letter.

Instructional Input

1. Reread the poems and have students identify each poem's rhyme scheme (AABBA).

2. Chart student responses on the chalkboard.

3. Reread the poems again. Invite students to clap or tap out the rhythm. If possible, provide students with rhythm instruments.

Guided Practice

1. Display the overhead transparency of the limericks from page 49.

2. Read the poems aloud while students identify the rhyme and rhythm. As you read, emphasize the stress on the second, fifth, and eighth syllables of the first, second, and fifth lines. These are the accented syllables.

3. Select one of the student samples to rewrite with your class following these procedures:

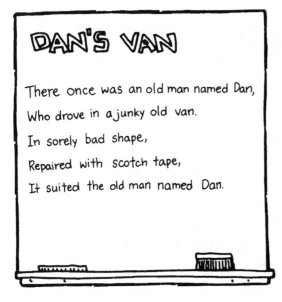

DAN'S VAN

There once was an old man named Dan,
Who drove in a junky old van.
In sorely bad shape,
Repaired with scotch tape,
It suited the old man named Dan.

a. Change the character or place in line 1. For example, *There once was a dancer named Anna* becomes *There once was a runner named Tim.*

b. Create a cluster by brainstorming words that rhyme with the name you selected in line 1. For example:

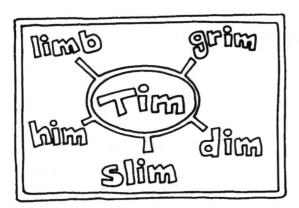

c. Create a new line 2 that rhymes with line 1 by choosing a word from the cluster to be the last word of the line. During guided practice, change only the key words of the limerick you are rewriting. For example:

Line 1: *There once was a runner named Tim,*
Line 2: *Who ran with his kitten named Slim.*

d. Create two shorter rhyming lines based on an activity or object that relates to the character(s). For example:

Line 3: *The two of them raced,*
Line 4: *Until they were chased,*

e. Write a fifth line, choosing an ending word from the cluster. (This line should rhyme with lines 1 and 2.) Line 5 can repeat words from lines 1 and 2. For example:

Line 5: *By a dog much bigger than Slim.*

4. As a class, rewrite several sample poems until students feel comfortable with the rhyme and rhythm pattern of limericks.

Independent Practice

1. Have students select partners.

2. Provide students with the Limerick Frame on page 50 and invite them to write original limericks. You may also want to provide students with a topic or suggest a first line.

Presentation

- Have students type up their limericks on computers and print them out. Invite them to illustrate their limericks. Then, compile the poems into a class book titled *Limerick Anthology.*

- All children enjoy listening to limericks because of the humorous, and at times outrageous, elements. Arrange for your class to visit another class to share their original limericks. The visit could conclude with the presentation of the *Limerick Anthology* created by your class.

- Each year, Castlemoyle Books sponsors a limerick contest. All entries must be received by May 12 of the year of the contest. Entries received after May 12 will be held for next year's contest. Entries are judged on creativity, originality, and adherence to the limerick format. Invite students to submit original limericks to this contest. For more information write to

Castlemoyle Books
15436 42nd Avenue South
Seattle, WA 98188
Fax: (206) 244-5382

Teaching Hints/Extensions

- Encourage students to work together to create cooperative progressive limericks. A progressive limerick is a series of limerick stanzas that create a story. Divide the class into small groups, with each group creating an initial limerick. The initial limerick is then passed to the next group to write a limerick that continues the theme and the characters. As the limerick passes from group to group, a humorous story emerges.

- Edward Leer's limericks often include the poetic device of alliteration (a string of words with the same initial sound), such as *The comfortable, confident cow.* As you read aloud Leer's limericks, have your class conduct an alliteration hunt, searching for other alliterative examples.

Limerick Samples

• Forty-Niner •
Student Author: Noah Bogart

There was once a forty-niner,
Who panned for gold as a miner.
Looking for gold,
He grew very old.
So instead he opened a diner.

• Young Dancer •
Student Author: Evie Christensen

There was a dancer named Anna,
Who danced with her dog Banana.
The two of them twirled,
Until they were hurled,
Right out of the house of Anna.

• Dan's Van •
Student Author: Brendan White

There once was an old man named Dan,
Who drove in a junky old van.
In sorely bad shape,
Repaired with Scotch tape,
It suited the old man named Dan.

• Plain Jane •
Student Author: Rebekah Sargent

There was a young girl from Maine,
Who drove her poor mother insane.
She cut off her hair,
And wrestled a bear.
She was, by no means, a plain Jane!

• Bare Hair •
Student Author: Joel Encarnacion

There once were some men with no hair,
Whose sore heads were shiny and bare.
They went through much pain,
But still couldn't gain,
A look that would give them some flair.

Limerick Frame

1. Choose the name of a character or place to use in the first line of your limerick.

_____

2. Create a cluster of words that rhyme with your character or place.

3. Write lines 1 and 2 of your limerick. Make sure these lines rhyme and have the same number of syllables.

Line 1:_____ (8 syllables)

Line 2:_____ (8 syllables)

4. Think of an activity or object that relates to your topic. Write two short rhyming lines concerning this.

Line 3:_____ (5 syllables)

Line 4:_____ (5 syllables)

5. Refer back to your cluster (step 2) and write a final line that rhymes with and has the same number of syllables as lines 1 and 2.

Line 5:_____ (8 syllables)

6. Read your limerick aloud. Make any necessary adjustments.

7. Recopy and illustrate your limerick.

Expressive Writing © 1998 Creative Teaching Press

Writer's Name: _____   Evaluator's Name: _____

Limerick Rubric

	Great!	O.K.	Needs Help
Critical Components			
Contains humorous or light-hearted subject matter			
Is composed of five lines and follows the correct rhyme pattern (AABBA)			
Follows the appropriate rhythm and syllable count			
Style			
Strong, active verbs			
Precise words			
Words that evoke images and express sensory detail			
Writing devices such as alliteration, metaphor, simile, onomatopoeia, and personification			
Originality			
Mechanics			
Ending punctuation			
Capitalization			
Comma rules			
Quotation marks			

Comments

_____

_____

_____

_____

Haiku

Critical Components

A haiku contains vivid words and phrases that describe nature. A haiku communicates thoughts and/or feelings. A haiku consists of 17 unrhymed syllables organized into three lines as follows:

Line 1: 5 syllables
Line 2: 7 syllables
Line 3: 5 syllables

Preparation

Bring to class haiku and nature poetry books such as *Cricket Never Does* by Myra Cohn Livingston, *Wind in the Long Grass* edited by William Higginson, or *In the Eyes of the Cat* translated by Tze-si Huang. Make an overhead transparency of page 55. Photocopy pages 56 and 57 for students. Have students look through magazines, calendars, and greeting cards to find nature pictures.

Setting the Stage

Read aloud several haiku poems. Inform students that haiku poetry was developed in Japan in the 1600s. Explain that the emperor of Japan would hold a contest to see who could compose the best haiku poem. The contest still exists today, with thousands of entries each year.

Instructional Input

1. Tell students that the purpose of a haiku poem is to create a word picture—a glimpse into nature, captured in precise, vivid words. These words cause the reader to feel or think about the scene described.

2. Reread each haiku poem and have students record (in words or quick sketches) the mental images each poem produced as well as any thoughts or feelings they had while listening. Chart student responses on the board.

3. Reread each poem again, instructing students to listen for syllable structure. Guide the class in clapping out each syllable. Ask *How many syllables in line 1?* (Five) *In line 2?* (Seven) *In line 3?* (Five) Record these findings on the chart.

Guided Practice

1. Display the overhead transparency of page 55. Cover the bottom half of the page.

2. Invite each student to work with a partner to copy the first line of one of the poems and invent second and third lines to complete it.

3. When students have completed their haiku, uncover the original poems and compare how your students' versions compared to the originals.

4. Write a class haiku following these procedures:

   • Select a nature picture or an actual natural object (for example, a flower, a shell, or an interesting piece of tree bark).

   • Brainstorm words or phrases that describe the mental images you want to produce.

   • Brainstorm words or phrases that tell when or where this is happening.

   • Brainstorm words or phrases that describe thoughts or feelings about the picture or object.

   • Select words from these lists to use in developing a three-line poem. (At this stage, stress the ideas and mental images produced, not the syllable count.) For example:

Beautiful lonely flower

Announcing spring's arrival

Rejoicing in Earth's rebirth

   • Adjust or modify the words to fit the 5-7-5 haiku syllable pattern. Try to include writing devices such as alliteration and personification. Title the poem.

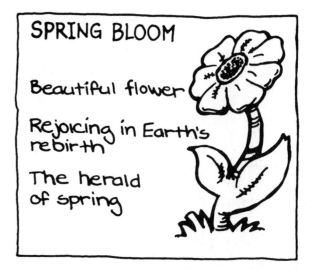

Independent Practice

1. Have each student select a nature picture or a natural object.

2. Have students develop their own haiku using the format modeled during guided practice. The Haiku Frame on page 56 can be used to assist students.

Presentation

- Have students create watercolor or pastel pictures to complement their poems. Then students can write their poems in permanent black marker on or above the picture. Mount the artwork and haiku on black construction paper or make it into banners to be displayed in the classroom, hallway, office, or home.

- As students share their completed haiku poems with the class or in small groups, remind each class member to note the mental image and feelings produced. Invite students to record these on index cards and give them to the author. These can later be posted near the displayed poem.

Teaching Hints/Extensions

- Many classic haiku poems focus on the seasons of the year. Divide your class into four groups and make each group responsible for creating a poem that focuses on a season. Have groups record and illustrate the poems on large pieces of poster board or butcher paper. The visual image of the changing seasons can, for example, be represented by four pictures of a tree that changes with each season.

- Tanka poems are similar to haiku but have two additional lines of seven syllables each (a total of 31 syllables). Tanka means "short song" in Japanese. Tanka was the most popular poetry in ancient Japan and an important aspect of Japanese courtship rituals. Invite students to write haiku poems and create related tanka responses, or have them trade poems with a partner. The tanka format is as follows:

Line 1: 5 syllables
Line 2: 7 syllables
Line 3: 5 syllables
Line 4: 7 syllables
Line 5: 7 syllables

Haiku Samples

• Windstorm •
Student Author: Nathan Christensen

Harsh, furious wind

_____

_____

• The Rainbow's Light •
Student Author: Allison Steele

Rainbows of light beams

_____

_____

• Hawaiian Evening •
Student Author: Julian Cisneros

Fiery sunset

_____

_____

• Wild River •
Student Author: Emily Windham

Wild, dancing river

_____

_____

• Windstorm •
Student Author: Nathan Christensen

Harsh, furious wind
Whipping, thrashing, and howling
Leaving destruction

• Hawaiian Evening •
Student Author: Julian Cisneros

Fiery sunset
Warm, sparkling, dancing water
Soft, rustling palm trees

• The Rainbow's Light •
Student Author: Allison Steele

Rainbows of light beams
Flooding shimmering colors
Across the blue sky

• Wild River •
Student Author: Emily Windham

Wild, dancing river
Sparkling, fresh, pure, free, and clean
Rushing and splashing

Expressive Writing © 1998 Creative Teaching Press

Haiku Frame

1. Select a topic. You may use a picture or object to provide ideas.

_____

2. Brainstorm words or phrases that describe the mental images you want to communicate.

_____

3. Brainstorm words or phrases that describe where or when this could be happening.

_____

4. Brainstorm words or phrases that describe thoughts or feelings you have about your topic.

_____

5. Write a three-line poem that creates a strong mental image of your topic. Include words or phrases from your lists.

_____

_____

_____

6. Adjust your poem to fit the haiku format.

_____ (5 syllables)

_____ (7 syllables)

_____ (5 syllables)

Expressive Writing © 1998 Creative Teaching Press

Writer's Name: _____   Evaluator's Name: _____

Haiku Rubric

	Great!	O.K.	Needs Help
Critical Components			
Contains descriptive words and phrases that describe nature			
Communicates thoughts and/or feelings			
Follows the three-line, 17-syllable format (5-7-5)			
Style			
Strong, active verbs			
Precise words			
Words that evoke images and express sensory detail			
Writing devices such as alliteration, metaphor, simile, onomatopoeia, and personification			
Originality			
Mechanics			
Ending punctuation			
Capitalization			
Comma rules			
Quotation marks			

Comments

_____

_____

_____

_____

Expressive Writing © 1998 Creative Teaching Press

Diamonte

Critical Components

A diamonte focuses on two opposite or contrasting subjects. A diamonte is arranged in seven lines that form a diamond pattern. A diamonte is composed of 16 words arranged in the following grammatical format:

Line 1: one noun

Line 2: two adjectives describing line 1

Line 3: three participles (-ing words) describing line 1

Line 4: four nouns—the first two relate to line 1, the second two relate to line 7

Line 5: three participles describing line 7

Line 6: two adjectives describing line 7

Line 7: one noun (the opposite of, or contrasting with, the noun in line 1)

Preparation

Make an overhead transparency of page 61. Photocopy pages 61–63 for students. Bring in the book *Opposites* by Richard Wilbur.

Setting the Stage

Read aloud several of Richard Wilbur's delightful rhyming poems about opposites. Tell students that they will also be writing about opposites using a poetry style called diamonte.

Instructional Input

1. Tell students that diamonte means "diamond" and that it is a special type of seven-line poem arranged in the shape of a diamond.

2. Write the requirements of the seven-line diamonte format on the board. Stress that diamonte poems are developed around two opposite or two contrasting nouns.

3. Brainstorm with students pairs of opposite words and chart these responses on the board.

4. Discuss the difference between opposite and contrasting words (contrasting words do not have the exact opposite meaning but they are significantly different).

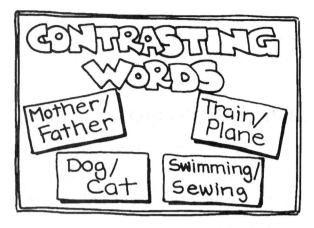

5. Brainstorm pairs of contrasting words and chart these responses on the board.

6. Read aloud the sample poem "Summer/Winter" on page 61. Discuss the parts of speech used for each line.

7. Have students brainstorm words that could replace those the author used. Ask students to determine the transition point in the poem when the subject changes from summer to winter (line 4 after the second noun).

Guided Practice

1. Read aloud another diamonte from page 61. As you read, have students stand or raise their hand when you reach the transition point of the poem.

2. Read aloud four more sample poems, omitting lines 1 and 7 each time. Challenge students to determine (based on lines 2–6) the missing subjects in each poem.

3. Record on the chalkboard the first three lines and the first half of line 4 of the remaining poem. Have students use the Diamonte Frame (page 62) for reference

and work with partners to create a second half of the poem. Invite students to share their completed poems with the class.

4. Distribute copies of pages 61 and 63. Ask students to use the Diamonte Rubric (page 63) to evaluate their favorite diamonte.

Independent Practice

1. Ask students to select a pair of opposite or contrasting words. (Remind them to refer to the previously made lists.)

2. Have students make a three-column chart for each word. Have them title the columns *Nouns, Adjectives,* and *Participles.*

3. Have students independently brainstorm and record several words for each column on their two charts.

4. Have students use the Diamonte Frame and their word charts to write their own diamonte poems.

Presentation

• Have each student write a diamonte about two of his or her hobbies or interests. Bind these into a diamond-shaped class book titled *Room _____'s Dynamite Diamontes.* Encourage students to record their names on the back of the poem rather than the front, so classmates can guess the author of each poem.

- Invite students to illustrate the two subjects of their diamonte on the top and bottom halves of a sheet of white construction paper. (For illustrating, watercolors, oil pastels, and crayons work best.) Then, have students copy their poems in pencil in the middle of the paper. Finally, have them write over the pencil in fine-point black marker. Encourage students to position the poem so line 4 is aligned with the intersection of the two illustrations. Arrange finished work on a bulletin board display.

Teaching Hints/Extensions

- Have each student select two animals that could represent contrasting aspects of their own character or personality. After brainstorming similarities between themselves and their chosen animals, invite students to write a diamonte describing these similarities. For example:

Monkey
Playful, funny
Scampering, running, laughing
Friends, activity, solitude, rest
Waiting, growling, hibernating
Slow, deliberate
Bear

Diamonte Samples

• Summer/Winter •
Student Author: Ryan Caro

Summer
Hot, green
Swimming, playing, resting
Insects, fruit, snow, rain
Skiing, sledding, hibernating
Cold, white
Winter

• Train/Airplane •
Student Author: Preston Hare

Train
Fast, large
Chugging, steaming, traveling
Rail, caboose, wing, jet
Flying, soaring, zooming
Swift, sleek
Airplane

• Surfing/Skateboarding •
Student Author: David Stough

Surfing
Fun, extreme
Exciting, thrilling, challenging
Wave, surfboard, asphalt, wheels
Riding, jumping, grinding
Cool, fast
Skateboarding

• Math/Spelling •
Student Author: Katrina Ford

Math
Orderly, logical
Working, thinking, knowing
Arithmetic, fractions, letters, words
Learning, writing, memorizing
Correct, fun
Spelling

• Pegasus/Unicorn •
Student Author: Katrina Ford

Pegasus
Smart, pretty
Flying, running, playing
Horse, wings, horn, pony
Galloping, wishing, racing
Magical, clever
Unicorn

• Desert/Mountain •
Student Author: Ryan Caro

Desert
Red, hot
Burning, drying, blistering
Dunes, sand, snow, forest
Towering, rising, refreshing
Cold, white
Mountain

Diamonte Frame

Line 1: one noun

Line 2: two adjectives describing line 1

Line 3: three participles (-ing words) describing line 1

Line 4: four nouns—the first two relating to line 1, the second two relating to line 7

Line 5: three participles (-ing words) describing line 7

Line 6: two adjectives describing line 7

Line 7: one noun

(the opposite of, or contrasting with, the noun in line 1)

Write Your Own Diamonte

_____

noun

_____   _____

adjective   adjective

_____   _____   _____

participle   participle   participle

_____ _____ _____ _____

noun   noun   noun   noun

_____   _____   _____

participle   participle   participle

_____   _____

adjective   adjective

_____

noun

Expressive Writing © 1998 Creative Teaching Press

Writer's Name: _____   Evaluator's Name: _____

Diamonte Rubric

	Great!	O.K.	Needs Help
Critical Components			
Focuses on two opposite or contrasting subjects			
Composed of seven lines arranged in a diamond pattern			
Contains appropriate parts of speech in the 16-word format			
Style			
Strong, active verbs			
Precise words			
Words that evoke images and express sensory detail			
Writing devices such as alliteration, metaphor, simile, onomatopoeia, and personification			
Originality			
Mechanics			
Capitalization			
Comma rules			
Quotation marks			

Comments

_____

_____

_____

_____

Bibliography

Professional Resource Books

Batzle, Janine. *Portfolio Assessment and Evaluation*. Creative Teaching Press, 1992.

Elbow, Peter. *Writing with Power: Techniques for Mastering the Writing Process*. Oxford, 1981.

Flynn, Kris. *Graphic Organizers*. Creative Teaching Press, 1995.

Graves, Donald H. *A Fresh Look at Writing*. Heinemann, 1994.

McCarthy, Tara. *150 Thematic Writing Activities*. Scholastic, 1993.

Miller, Wilma H. *Alternative Assessment Techniques for Reading & Writing*. Center for Applied Research in Education, 1995.

Schifferle, Judith. *Editorial Skills*. Center for Applied Research in Education, 1985.

Schifferle, Judith. *Word Skills*. Center for Applied Research in Education, 1985.

Sparks, J.E. *Write for Power*. Communication Associates, 1995.

Sunflower, Cherlyn. *Really Writing! Ready-to-Use Writing Process Activities for the Elementary Grades*. Center for Applied Research in Education, 1994.

Young, Sue. *Scholastic Rhyming Dictionary*. Scholastic, 1997.

Character Sketches

Krull, Kathleen and Kathryn Hewitt. *Lives of the Artists*. Harcourt Brace Jovanovich, 1992.

Krull, Kathleen and Kathryn Hewitt. *Lives of the Musicians*. Harcourt Brace Jovanovich, 1993.

Krull, Kathleen and Kathryn Hewitt. *Lives of the Writers*. Harcourt Brace Jovanovich, 1994.

Diamontes

Wilbur, Richard. *Opposites*. Harcourt Brace Jovanovich, 1991.

Haiku

Higginson, William (editor). *Wind in the Long Grass*. Simon and Schuster, 1991.

Huang, Tze-si (translator). *In the Eyes of the Cat*. Holt, 1994.

Lewis, Patrick J. *Black Swan, White Crow*. Simon and Schuster, 1995.

Livingston, Myra Cohn. *Cricket Never Does*. McElderry Books, 1997.

Journals

Stevens, Carla. *A Book of Your Own: Keeping a Diary or Journal*. Clarion, 1993.

Frank, Anne. *Anne Frank: The Diary of a Young Girl*. Bantam, 1993.

Roosevelt, Theodore. *The Roosevelt Diaries of Boyhood and Youth*. Scribner, 1928.

Sloane, Eric. *The Diary of an Early American Boy*. Ballantine, 1974.

Limericks

Ciardi, John. *The Hopeful Trout and Other Limericks*. Houghton Mifflin, 1992.

Leer, Edward. *The Nonsense Verse of Edward Leer*. Harmony Books, 1984.

Livingston, Myra Cohn. *Lots of Limericks*. McElderry, 1991.

Lobel, Arnold. *The Book of Pigericks*. HarperTrophy, 1988.

Rosenbloom, Joseph. *The Looniest Limerick Book in the World*. Derrydale, 1991.

Quatrains

Ferris, Helen. *Favorite Poems Old and New*. Doubleday, 1957.

Prelutsky, Jack. *The New Kid on the Block*. Greenwillow, 1994.

Prelutsky, Jack. *The Random House Book of Poetry for Children*. Random House, 1983.

Silverstein, Shel. *A Light in the Attic*. Harpercrest, 1987.

Silverstein, Shel. *Where the Sidewalk Ends*. Harpercrest, 1987.

Wilbur, Richard. *Opposites*. Harcourt Brace Jovanovich, 1973.

Similes

Wood, Audrey. *Quick As a Cricket*. Child's Play, 1982.

Juster, Norton. *As: A Surfeit of Similes*. Morrow, 1989.